Megan's Thoughts

of Motivation

VOLUME 2

BY **Megan McGlover**

ISBN: 978-1-60414-975-3

Visit her website:

www.MeganLMcGlover.com

www.justiceforwandamcglover.com

Contents

Introduction .... *v*
Acknowledgments .... *vii*
Dedication .... *ix*

A Beautiful Surprise 1
Bend Don't Break 2
Accept The Impossible 3
Good Vibrations 4
Do You Trust You? 5
Dream! 6
What's Attractive To You? 7
Comfort Zone 8
Don't Hide 9
Persistence 10
Obviously Compassionate 11
ITs Purpose 12
Be Yourself Without Being Yourself 13
Find the Good 14
The Closet! 15
This Might Be Your 40-Day Fast 16
Tithe Yourself 17
Affirm It! 18

Feelings Without Foundation 19
Wasted Ts 20
What You Hear 21
New Endings 22
Workout Daily 23
Never Sorry 24
Who is Your God? 25
PC to a MAC 26
"I just, I can't, I just, can't be..." 27
This Will Be Simple and Sweet… 28
Be Grateful for the Dirt 29
Believe in Your Vision 30
Peace You Can't Buy 31
Misery Loves Company 32
Don't Shut Out Change 33
I Want to Get Accustomed to Heaven 34
Now! 34
Let It Go! 35
Stretch! 36
Integrity 37
When Will Your Enoch Come? 38
The Fullest Expression of Myself 39
Divine Intentions Lead to Divine Interventions 40

Take a Step Towards Your Fear 41
Know Your Buttons 42
"No man can run from his own story" 43
Creating a Reality That Never Happened 44
It *Will* Pass 45
Be Anxious For Nothing… 46
What's the Cure 47
Blessing Me Right NOW! 48
Generational Curse 49
Keep It High 50
God's Will? 51
I'm Encouraged 52
Stand for You 53
Do You Cuss When You Pray? 54
Stranded 55
Don't Be Afraid of Freedom 56
Give It Up Turn It Loose 57
Be Quiet and Listen 58
Forgive Yourself 59
You Gotta Trim the Fat 60
Pat Yourself 61
Did I Get Caught Up?! 62

I Love You Long and I Love You Strong

It is an honor and a great pleasure to present you with my first published book, *Megan's Thoughts,* a brief journey through my mind, my thoughts and the self-interpretation of such.

This is not a religious book in anyway. It is however, a Spiritual book that people from all walks of life can enjoy.

We (you and I) talk here about; Love, trusting oneself, the avenues of the soul, precious moments, weight concerns, family life and certainly the God within.

Oh Glory Be, to the Highest and He who reigns in Me. Do we believe that Spirit is all about us... amongst us and within us? Do we know that the Supreme Knowledge not only has the answers but makes them available to us? Do we really believe in that greater good that abides so consciously? Do we really know? I hope to answer these questions here.

Take a look inside and find your Freedom...

Acknowledgments

With complete gratitude I would like to acknowledge Angels that I have in my life:

My Mother, Wanda McGlover

My Sister, Adrianne

My True Friends

My Editor, Alicen Harmon

My Ancestors and their prayers which are still manifesting.

I want to humbly thank mySelf for not giving up... Thank You!

And to My God!

This Book of My Thoughts is Dedicated in Love to:

Eva Bradford-Rock,
My only grandparent and marvelous author. She will always be a powerhouse and an example of a marvelous woman;

Ms. Rose Montero,
A counselor to counselors. You changed my life;

A Beautiful Surprise

Who remembers the rapid heartbeat, HUGE smile and the beads of joy rolling down your face... as you walked through the door of your surprised birthday party? Or better yet, who remembers the day you walked into your master suite and found the person you love had placed rose petals all over the room... OH, better yet, who remembers the moment they experienced peace... true peace?

I'm sure when we review the thoughts we had as children, we had no idea that as adults we would talk, think or even live as we do. We never envisioned such stress, misunderstanding, unpaid bills and emotional unpleasantries. We hoped, if nothing else, that we would evolve into the fairy tales of "LaLa Land"... living happily ever after. However, it seems like the moment that story book closed, so did that fantastic resolve. BUT we can still anticipate the surprise.

See, a surprise is something we don't know is coming. Well we can always feel it, someone always hints about it... sometimes people slip up and tell us. But still, we're not completely sure, we just stay open to the idea.

I think that as we've gotten older we've outgrown the element of surprise; the blessing in the miracle, the hope in the faith. We've become too serious, too jaded and way too controlling. Loosen up, live free and relax... there might be a crowd of people on the other side and you don't want them to see you frowning.

The best gifts come as surprises... beautiful surprises. But we have to be open to receive them or they will never be revealed.

Bend Don't Break

"Be flexible with your methods not your mission." Is this not one of thee most wonderful things you›ve ever heard? I found it Earth moving! See, your mission, your destiny is not up for compromise. This is our purpose, that thing that makes you You, that thing that makes your confidence appear almost cocky… because you›re just that sure. It (that thing) is not up for discussion. This is why it is so important that we take time out to find out what our purpose is. Most of us already know, perhaps out of fear we don›t DO, but we have a pretty good idea of what Spirit has placed on our heart. But without knowing for sure, we stand the risk of flexibility altering our destiny.

How we go about living within our purpose is our methodand that simply shows maturity. We must recognize that our ways are not the only ways and change brings progress. I›m sure that it is not our destiny to be stubborn. LOL So the road that we take, the car we›ve been placed in to travel that road, may need some adjustment or tune-ups however; that final destination at the end of this road trip should not be compromised by a popularity contest.

That really did wonders for my Spirit, I hope it has blessed you too. You can handle it!

BOOM!

Accept The Impossible

I heard someone say something that blew my dreads back. He said with confidence," The things that God does in your life will be so BIG, that it>s going to frighten you!r Well without giving all the details, I ended up laid out on the floor that day, completely overwhelmed by that confirmation.

Just a few days prior I wrote on my blog about NEW-ness. Being grateful for the newness of mind, understandings, peace, etc. I decided that what I see as being a wonderful, majestic life, is just the very tip of what is already Universally predestined... we just have to get out of our own way and allow God to have our backs. Don>t allow fear of the unknown to hold you back from that pure greatness that is already YOU!

I>ve said aloud," Spirit I am grateful for what I don>t even know, I just know You got my back.r

Today is the day we no longer define our blessings by fear - Today we accept the impossible!

So let's ride today out with a smile.

Good Vibrations

Think about perception and the energy we send out into the universe. Iím a firm believer that our thoughts attract and shape our reality. So, briefly today, think about what youíre thinking about. Notice how it makes you feel.

Notice where the thought is coming from and why youíre thinking that way. Are these thoughts bringing us closer to the good that we know we are... and the good that we expect from Spirit, the Universe?

I've mentioned before that this is similar to the Buddhist explanation of meditation — conscious thought. Being aware of that which transfers in your mind.

Today let's try it, feel what you're thinking: And if it doesnít feel good (if your feelings don't have proper foundation) then change your thought — change your vibration.

Do You Trust You?

I have yet another question... Do people influence you more then you influence them? What I mean by this is, when you have a thought particularly about yourself or something youíre going through, do you hold to that or allow other peopleís perceptions change how and what you think about yourself?

I told someone this week, "The reason why you're confused right now is because you have become detached from your Spirit and can not recognize your own voice." This goes back to spending time alone, being honest with yourself and God and dealing directly with YOURSELF.

Someone once told me that I needed to learn to trust myself. I thought it was crazy at first, then I realized what they meant. 1. Do I have my best interest at heart? 2. Am I clear about my purpose and making decisions based on that purpose? 3. Do I honor and respect myself... treating myself as if in a relationship with myself? (That's a deep one; think about it.) 4. Would I place myself in harms way?

These questions sound crazy right? But they are serious. Once you trust yourself you will believe not only in yourself.... But you will BELIEVE YOU!

Take a moment and answer those questions. Let's see what we accomplish.

Dare to Dream!

"God does not give us vision with out provision." We all have dreams and great hopes for our lives, right? But do you believe it is possible? Some of us want to loose weight, be a doctor, finish school, have a good marriage... but do we believe in it so much that we actually **TAKE THE STEPS TOWARD ITS FULFILLMENT?**

I think that we have a tendency to wait for a miraculous Earth Shaking jumpstart to our success. In the meantime, we waste precious opportunities.

When we take the first step towards manifesting our dreams, we alert the Universe to our belief that, **"YES I want this and believe I shall have it!"**

A dream is simply a vision waiting to be accepted, affected and actualized. **So whatever it is that You want for You start today and go GET IT! One step at a time.**

What's Attractive To You?

I wonder how upset people will be with me after this statement ... What percentage of the drama in our lives is our fault? How much of the negative that we receive has to do with the negative we put out? What do you mean Megan? We are attracting to us, whether we are conscious of it or not. What we feel, think, believe and perceive is sending energetic signals.

When we begin to change the inner most thought processes of our minds we will inevitably change the outer realms of our realities. For example, all of us have encountered that one someone at work that just burns the last nerve we have left, right? So when you get up in the morning that person is on your mind, "Now I got to go deal with this so and so..." In the car, we're thinking about this person, getting our coffee or tea... and God forbid if the person walks past us, the feeling of pure negative energy comes all over our presence. You are attracting that negative to you, because you have given your energy to it. It must be reversed! If and when you think about this person, think GOOD thoughts... "They will be nice today... I pray for their journey, their joy, their peace... I love this person." It sounds crazy, but it WORKS!

This same thought process should be adopted with all things: bills, family, friends and intimate relationships. Let's try it today. If nothing else, I promise you will feel much better.

Comfort Zone

Ok so we already know that we need to be comfortable with ourselves in order for us to be comfortable anywhere, right? Of course. But I was thinking the other day, how often we find ourselves in a situation or place that we're not comfortable in. For example, we tell our teenage girls (and boys), don't let anyone force you into having sex before you're ready... but then they see us being forced to do things we don't want to do all the time. We have friends that aren't really our friends, we stay in abusive relationships, we mistreat our bodies (health wise), we complain about work, time, God, the list goes on and on... The mirror we're presenting isn't very clear.

Comfort is a choice, so get comfortable. It is not your destiny to be miserable, I promise.

Don't Hide

Do you notice that when we feel bad about ourselves we begin to withdraw? When we see ourselves as "less than" to a degree, we retreat into our caves. When we have a hint of depression, we run further into that dark place... Well STOP IT!

I've noticed that as time ages, disappointment will go from an opportunity to make things better, to a complete death sentence. What do I mean? For example, if someone is overweight they are not included, they are taught to feel less than and society makes sure that they are so discouraged that trying to loose weight is worse then staying overweight... Therefore these persons continue to isolate themselves further and further away.

Unfortunately we cannot change our society overnight, but we CAN and WILL change our minds individually. If you have these thoughts about yourself change them. If you wear braces, are overweight, have acne, wear glasses and are single at age 40, whatever it is that makes you an INDIVDUAL. ... Embrace it. Embrace YOU! Once you begin to love yourself, you can see who you really are and make changes as YOU SEE FIT.

Persistence

Don't give up. We've heard the saying; "do it anyhow"... even when you don't want to do something, if you know it's something you should do... do it anyhow. Practice makes perfect, so perfectly practice. There will be things that come up to try and distract you from accomplishing your dreams. Notice them, recognize them and tackle them — but keep going.

Life is a journey that persists on the perception of our minds. When we know the root of something, we can take it with a grain of salt, apply it in a positive way and forge towards the mark of the high calling. That high calling is our true self, our true nature, that which we are called to be in the first place.

So don't give up, because when you do, you're giving up on You!

Obviously Compassionate

I've talked about having compassion for others and how you never know what someone is going through. But that is more internal than anything, right? What I mean by that is, compassion is usually something that we think about in our heads, but what about the things that we say. For example, someone may not be on your level at finding the good in everything. So when speaking to you, they may feel resentful or beneath your spiritual accomplishments. The point I'm trying to make is be obviously compassionate to others spiritual plain.

There's nothing worse than someone who is trying to help, stabbing you in the face with their overbearing sense of self. (LOL) Read that again, that was good. Love is gentle and kind, not trying to prove a point. Love accepts, respects and uplifts.

Love is Loving.

ITs Purpose

In my opinion to accept something is to acknowledge IT and appreciate IT for what IT is. It doesn't mean you "agree" with IT, but you can see IT's reason, grasp the experience and arrive at a greater self from IT's existence.

IT can be anything; a person (friend or foe, lover, spouse), a job, drama, personal issues (weight, attitude, mindset)... the list goes on. These ITS are in our lives for reasons. But if we're constantly fighting against IT because we don't agree, don't want to be rational, don't feel the need to stop and listen... we will never find out IT's purpose in our lives and therefore never be at peace.

Ok, let me say it this way. You have a friend who is drama-filled 99% of the time. She has 99 problems and common sense is not one of them. BUT you remain her friend. There is a reason (universal reason) for this. It could be a number of things:

1. You are developing patience.
2. There is a level of drama in your life that she reflects.
3. There is a lesson in it for her (from you).
4. God is punishing you. LOL (Seriously I don't believe in this at all!).

Instead of being overwhelmed by the current situations we're in, we should accept them with arms of energetic love, which transforms the whole reception process. (Oh I liked that, let's read that again). Once we let go of our defensive mechanisms, we can then see things multi-dimensionally (I think I just made that word up, but you get me, right?) ALL of this however does not mean that we don't make changes to better our lives! But how can we make change without knowing what or why we're changing in the first place? DEEP!

I think this is one of the definitions of God; He looks at the heart. He sees things from every possible angle – like the lesson before the trail.

Be Yourself Without <u>Being</u> Yourself

WOW having a New Life is not easy. We have to keep in mind that we are not supposed to "define" who we are, we are just supposed to BE who we already are. That can be very difficult when dealing with the egotistic mind or ego.

We have the human condition of wanting to be recognized as something or someone, not necessarily "famous" someone, but the ego wants to be noticed. Therefore we seek to define ourselves through something identifiable. I am a teacher, writer, doctor, actress, comedian, victim; the list goes on.

I guess what I'm saying is let's be ourselves; without being ourselves. Live and let live. When we see life in someone else, congratulate it and applaud yourself for recognizing freedom in someone else.

It can be difficult just trying to relax... but let's give it a shot, shall we?

Find the Good

Anyone over the age of 2 years old knows that we don't always get what we want, things don't always go our way and life is not always a bowl of cherries. As adults we can look back over our lives and reflect on some real hardships and disappointments through our journey thus far. We recognize that in the grand scheme of things we are all creations that create and have the ability to change and redirect with the power of our perception(s).

But what about those times when you're smack dead in the middle of crap? Yep, crap! But really what do you do?

You find the good crap. (LOL I crack myself up.) But that's really it. You must find the good. If we believe in an all-powerful Spirit who created us in His image, our lives and that journey within always has good in it somewhere... because the Creator is only good... Am I right? Yes I Am.

FIND THE GOOD

in whatever it is — capitalize on it, transform it, learn from it, and

KNOW it. BOOM!

Have an awesome day...you're looking for the good, right?

Obviously.

The Closet!

"Judge not, lest you be judged."
— BIBLE

Now we got that outta the way here's my take. I am actually more sympathetic to this issue then most may think. As most of the world may already know, Bishop Eddie Long was accused of misusing his pastoral position and having contact of a sexual nature with 4 particular young men. Although it did not go to trial and long denied the accusations, a settlement of $25 Million dollars was reached. As you may know, if you follow me on Youtube, I don't really enjoy speaking on the person directly, I try to look at the situation in a way that we can all get a lesson out of it. You know what I mean?

So let's talk about the closet. We've heard the saying, "What's in the closet will always come to light" and "Your skeletons will one day come out of the closet"... and so on. But we never really talk about the closet itself. This dark, usually very small, tight, uncomfortable, unforgiving box that holds what others and we, deem as our most shameful secrets, it is, in and of itself, the shame that we try so desperately to hide. Shame, which I call the closet, tells us daily that we don't deserve to be loved, that we will never be good enough, that we are forever "doomed", that we are just so far off the mark it's too late. This shame keeps us from our true self, keeps us from our loved ones and keeps us locked in the closet.

The closet to me is like a cult. It is usually a group of people who are so miserable within themselves that they will basically believe anything as long as it takes the pressure off the real issue. Instead of taking the time out to massage the soul that is You, they choose to drink the Kool-Aid. So in the cases of these officials (Wiener, Schwarzenegger), pastors and persons in leadership who are constantly stepping all over the principles and morals of marriage and these standards they "hold in such great esteem", they rather force us in the closet with them instead of coming out dealing with the TRUTH and helping others come out as well.

It is not about your sexual preference or whether you cheat on your taxes, your diet or you're a closet-eater... this is about LOVING YOU. Whoever you are, whatever your desires, whatever your issues you deserve to be loved and that love must first start with you. It has been said and is true; "People will treat you according to how you treat yourself." Now I'm not saying tell all your business, I'm a private person, however I am saying deal with who you are... baggage and all... then embrace yourself. Because whatever you want to change you can. But Honey, you can't do it while you're in the closet there's simply not enough room.

This Might Be Your 40-Day Fast

When we're in the midst of trials and tribulations, it can be very difficult to see the purpose and/or reason for them... especially when the circumstances cause us to be alone. You know what I mean? Those times in our lives when we feel completely alone and friends are gone, or can't be counted on, family is gone and you're in tears more often then not... and you feel like you're out there all by yourself.

A friend of mine called me for some Spiritual advice the other day about a guy that they like… and how much they didn't understand why it's taking sooooooo long, etc. My response, in short was; "Perhaps this is your 40-day fast". When Jesus went into the mountains for 40 days/nights, he was there to prepare Himself for Greatness, for His PURPOSE.

If we look carefully at some of our situations, we will realize the same thing... We're preparing for our own greatness. 40-days may not be literal, your 40-days may be going on a year now: a year of celibacy, a year without work, a year without friends or family. It could be even longer. But know that you're going through the purification process to become the TRUE YOU!

And KNOW that you're never alone because you're always there. I like that.

Tithe Yourself

Someone told me this a while ago and it has always stuck with me... "Pay yourself a tithe." When I first became a personal trainer (getting paid for it, that is), a friend that I really look up to said, "Girl, give yourself 20% of everything you make." My first thought was, "It's all mine anyhow." But then it sunk in. Once it did, I found myself with $200, then $300 dollars in a jar without realizing it was accumulating so much.

So, what does this have to do with it being a cold and wet Tuesday? Glad you asked. Two things:

1. I feel it's very important to HONOR ourselves. It seems to me that we are not praising ourselves — yes, I said "praising ourselves" — enough. Do we really realize who we are? I think not. We are literally walking miracles. (Think about that...) There will nor has there ever been another YOU!
2. This "tithe money" is only for you — not the kids, the bills, the whatever (yes, even in this recession)! This money is for an hour-long massage, a mani-pedi, a session with your therapist, an accupuncture session ... the things that we all need to keep US aligned with our purpose.

This tithe is to help the temple of God function at its highest level. Doesn't that sound familiar?

Start today, even if it's just $1. Set aside something for your praise and worship. I know I'm stretching the perimeters of your minds ... but just go with me here.

Affirm It!

I was wondering if you think it's silly to write the words, "I am Beautiful" on the bathroom mirror. Or, place post-it notes throughout your house saying, "I'm successful", "I am prosperous"… How many of us really understand the power of affirmation? Affirmation is like driving a car, (just go with me!). If you're driving in the wrong direction, you simply turn. You may have to make several turns and U-turns, perhaps even drive into a parking lot and get your bearings, but eventually you're back on track. So when you get up in the morning feeling not your best, go into the bathroom and see a note "I am beautiful" you've made a turn in your mind, by affirming that which is true in your reality. WOW! That was deep.

Does this work in every aspect of life? I'd like to think so. Try telling yourself you WILL have a good day; then sit back and watch. The day's activities may be no different than they were before. However, your mindset has been altered to perceive everything in a more positive way. You know what I mean?

Last night before going to bed I certainly didn't feel my best, then I realized I have the power to change this. I began affirming. Well when I got up this morning, I felt the same way, BUT I just began changing my thought patterns. It's a journey, right? So let's think on those things, which are good! … And we're in this together.

FEELINGS WITHOUT FOUNDATION

Don't be too concerned with how you feel: move in what you know. But, wait what do we know? That's the tricky part, right? It seems like we get entangled in what we feel; But our feelings aren't really based on what we know; and what we do know isn't grounded... Therefore the emotions (that we're reacting off of) are not thorough. Sometimes they're simply misunderstood, mistaken or misinterpreted all together.

What if we took the time out to find out (study) what we believe and get to know ourselves better? What would be unveiled if we got to know the simple things like what we really want in life? What happens when we become really honest with ourselves? (Not questions but statements).

I hope we all take the time today to sit with our Spirit and get to know the basis of our emotions and feelings. Some are deep and will take time. So where do we start? By making a choice. That's the first step to ANYTHING.

Wasted Ts

TIME · TALENT · TREASURES

A friend of mine said, "Potential means you're not doing anything now."- NL Hamilton. When I heard this I nearly collapsed! We all have potential but what are we doing with it? Each one of us possesses a gift(s) we are not tapping into, using or developing. We are wasting our time, talent and treasures.

I believe passion drives the soul: it gets you up in the morning: it transforms the negative into the positive because we are focused on the goal, not the strife. Faith (God's love for us) invested deeply into that which we are passionate about will revolutionize the very core of your world. When you thrust forward in confidence and courage, you can't lose.

Let's see our potential as tangible reality, not something we could be.

I believe in your belief in YOU.

Are you having a good day? You should be!

What You Hear

"Don't believe everything you hear." Easier said then done, right? Don't we have the tendency to over-hear sometimes? Even when we know the source is not the most reputable one, we still hold on to tidbits of "gossipy" information.

Taking what we hear with a grain of salt is not only wise, but healthy in many ways. Just like food, words are digested into our physique and can cause chemical re-actions, whether they are positive or negative. For example, when someone gets really upset, their blood pressure rises, they may began to sweat, hyperventilate or shake etc. — All this from getting upset or angry over something someone may have said to or about them.

So what am I saying? Don't digest everything you hear. Taking everything in is not always the healthiest choice. Listen intently for the good.

Love You Long, Love You Strong...

This week is a week of NEW Endings. We've heard time and time again about New Beginnings, right? Of course... but how can we start anew when we're still "fooling-around" with the old? On my last birthday I realized I am able to move forward only by leaving behind that which is no longer a part of my life journey.

Now certainly we can carry baggage around as long as we'd like; Spirit is not going to stop us. However, when we do this it gets harder and harder to go through the new doors of opportunity... and perhaps one day we wont make it through at all. Some things in our lives are no longer of any use to us; whether it be things, people, jobs, past emotional justifications (*uh oh*). Whatever it is, its purpose has come and gone and is no longer servicing our destiny which awaits us.

So as I look towards my future, I pray you'll all join me in looking towards yours as well. Then look in your suitcase and make sure you have what you need, because it costs extra when you over pack.

Let Go of the Old. Let's make life ROCK!

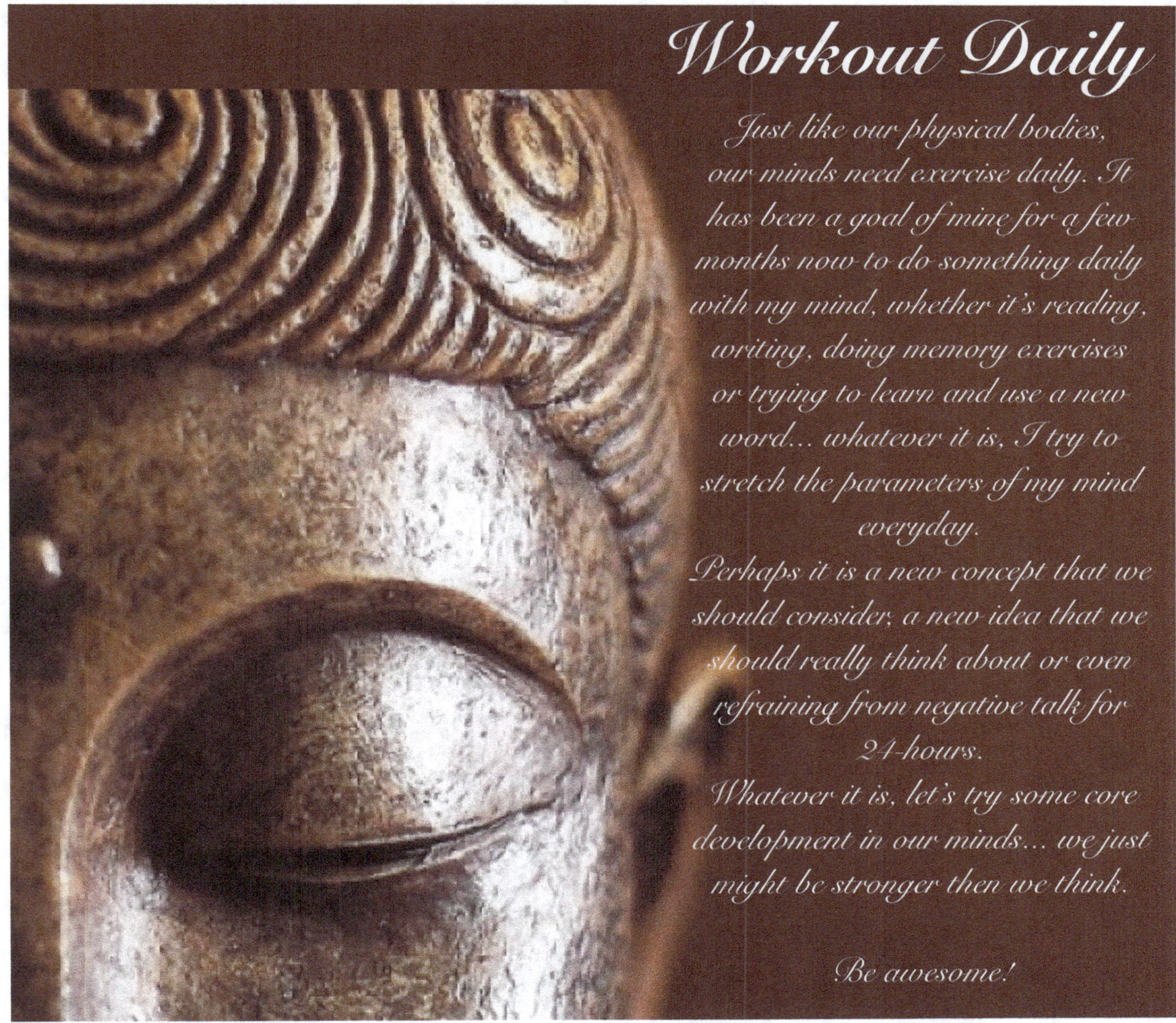
Workout Daily
Just like our physical bodies, our minds need exercise daily. It has been a goal of mine for a few months now to do something daily with my mind, whether it's reading, writing, doing memory exercises or trying to learn and use a new word... whatever it is, I try to stretch the parameters of my mind everyday.
Perhaps it is a new concept that we should consider, a new idea that we should really think about or even refraining from negative talk for 24-hours.
Whatever it is, let's try some core development in our minds... we just might be stronger then we think.
Be awesome!

Never Sorry

Life has granted me the blessing of knowing, the knowledge of wisdom and the blessing of simply being. So why would I apologize to the life of which I breathe? Why would I doubt the certainty that has been given, the assurance that has been assured? I won't, I never will again... for I AM. The blessed peace withstanding, the running over, the agape expression, I am the joy of that which I dream... I am its evolution.... Am I not?

I've always said, "It is my reality that counts...." Therefore my joy, my hopes, my dreams are actualized through me... Yep, the same goes for you too.

I learned to grieve today. I cried for reasons I was unsure of. I released myself to internal internal without inhabitation or judgment. I actually released myself INTO my feeling. NO, I did not evolve into a Buddha, but I did realize that it's ok; It's ok to feel, it's ok to be ME. WOW! I'm just now being me.... Completely – and I'm not sorry for who I AM!

Who is Your God?

My friend told me once, "Stop telling God how big your problems are; tell your problems how BIG your God is." Powerful words that we should live by, right? But I tweaked it just a little; tell your problems WHO your God is.

See I think that we have a tendency to make other things our gods, which inevitably become our problem(s). If you look at a situation that you're dealing with and research back just a little bit, I'm sure that we will all discover that there was a fork in the road where we made a choice based on our wants and Idol-I-listic (I just made that up) ideas. For example, your love life is shot (now) and when you look back, you'll see how you kept choosing the wrong type of person (then), because they "fit" your certain criteria. But when you look around and think things over... you see that your criteria (how they look, how much money they had, etc. ...) was not based on love but on something else (your idol). Right?

So today you're in the midst of a problem, tell it that it is no longer the focal point of your existence. Tell it that your decisions will now be based on Love, not greed. Tell it WHO your God really is.

BOOM!

PC to a MAC

My Boothang just purchased her first MACBOOK PRO!!!!!! YAY! Right... NOPE! All of you who jumped for joy were dead wrong. Why? Because she couldn't transfer her music! "OMG! This is one of the best computers that you can buy and you're upset because you can't transfer (readily) some music that's already on your iPod? Ok so you can't hear music at this moment." Sometime Joy takes time.

TWO POINTS:

#1 — We hang onto the past... way too much. I know this is a stretch but let's look at it. With the new operating system (new relationship, new job, new education, new computer, new understanding, new awareness) you DO have the ability to transfer your music (joy, happiness, evolved peace AND ALL) however it will take a little extra work. BUT once you do it, life is much easier, much more secure and much more musical.

#2 — ALL SHOULD NOT BE TRANSFERED! Yep I said that and I meant every word! Have you ever heard, "some things (people, places and even things) are here for a reason, a season and a lifetime? Same goes with change. Some changes are here to hurtle you into the movement of life.... some will remind you, constantly, of the JOY you once felt... and some go until Love fades.... which it never does.

As you make the exchange from despair to hope... between faith and fear.... between eternal joy and temporary ridiculousness.... remember YOU HAVE A CHOICE!

iLYL, iLYS

"I just, I can't, I just, can't be..."

I'm not the biggest P-Diddy fan on earth by no stretch, but this song does it for me! He's speaking of a relationship he was in and how he loved the person more then he loved himself and he just can't do it anymore... but the concept of the song is so deep! Well the concept is is deep to me. LOL

***"Anything that you love more then you love yourself
is a Dangerous Infatuation.
Money, sex, drugs, fame, whatever it is...
when you let your Spirit lay way-side to that which you find
so dauntingly provocative,
you spit in the face of your own existence."***

— MLM quote

Life is a journey not a trial. Regardless of what you've heard, trials come but they should not be the foundational component of your faith. Faith is NOT an overwhelming test of your love for God — (as I say, I'm talking real good). Faith is the PROOF of God's love for you.

So when you are face to face with that which you love more than you love yourself, weigh it against the love your KNOW God has for you. If you don't know what that equates to, grab a piece of paper and write down all you're grateful for... you'll get the idea.

This Will Be Simple and Sweet...

Love on yourself like you just found the person of your dreams and they are wining and dining you like the royalty you are. Imagine you have come and swept yourself off your feet, saved you from a day of issues and caressed your very woes with a gentle hand of confidence. Hug yourself passionately as if reuniting with your loved one in the airport after a long absence. Massage your thoughts, like a gentle whisper of kindness from your truest love during a rough day's work. Congratulate yourself for making it through yet another long week, by expressing aloud how proud you are of you...

Love on yourself, experience Love at its finest hour, its most precious interpretation.

Some of us have had quite a few ups and downs (emotionally)... now it's time to relax, for just a moment and recognize that jewel deep in the midst of our very existence.

Be Grateful for the Dirt

A Lotus flower (which I have tattooed on my arm) grows in mud... not just dirt that you can brush off, but nasty, slushy, stick to your skin until you wash it off, mud. The meaning of this beautiful Lotus in Buddhism is to understand the ongoing-ness of cause and effect AND to know, in simpler terms, you will become a flower even through the mud.

But it seems to me that the mud gets a bad rep. Well, what do you mean, Megan? I'm so glad that you asked. See, mud is a nutrient; it is the soil, it is the first mothering to your roots. Mud baths can make your skin beautiful, mud can make a hut: mud is the groundwork of human flesh (Remember Adam?). So to bring it around, when we look at the mud, the slushiness in our lives, think about what mud is helping us to become.

Respect even the mud in your life; it's making you grow more rapidly!

BE SOME BLESSED MUD FOR SOMEONE TODAY!

BELIEVE IN YOUR VISION

If you don't believe in it, what makes you think people are going to rally up and support it? Some of the happiest people on this planet are the ones that had the craziest ideas and went with it. They're the ones that had wild imaginations, thoughts and fantasies. They're the ones who had a strong passion for something that had never been done before.

We have been given gifts, all of us and we owe it to ourselves to use them in the fulfillment of our daily joys… don't you agree? Moses said, "A people without a vision will perish." I say, "A people who have a vision but don't believe in it are just walking in circles for 40 years!"

Peace You Can't Buy

My level of gratitude and appreciation leaped to new heights when I realized I have peace. Then when I became aware that peace is not just a feeling but a way of being.... my praise evolved into pure worship and dance. I suppose this is why I stress; "Be yourself.... Deal with the issues... Feel Joy.... Don't get hung up on the little things.... etc." - these topics and victories over them bring about a peace that cannot be explained... a peace that we should all attain.

When I heard the news that Amy Winehouse was found dead in her hotel room, my heart cried. The music that she produced with that awesome voice was simply good music, (something we don't have much of these days). But although I was hurt, I was so relieved for her. Sounds crazy but listen, that girl was awfully afraid to live true life and she had absolutely no peace.

It is important, so very important, that we continue to seek our truth, our purpose and our destiny. It is important that we take care of our feelings, our perspectives and our hearts. Because when we don't... it's simply sad.

Misery Loves Company

Now we do realize that misery loves company, right? I mean I don't have to spend an entire paragraph proving to you that those who are miserable like to have someone to bounce misery off of, right? Let me take it a little deeper... because that's me... Negativity is energy, same as Positivity. When someone comes to you and says, "OMG I just love your energy, your Spirit..." They're commenting on your positive energy that has attracted the positive-ness in them. Now, the same goes for the opposite of that. Negativity as an energy attracts the negative-ness in others. In Buddhism, particularly Nichren Diashonin Buddhism, it is said that there are equal parts (negative and positive) residing in our life conditions and it is your perspective and how you control those parts that brings complete happiness. Ok but without going all deep into that let's get back to the gut of this.

DUMP YO MISERABLE FRIENDS!

I hate to say it this way, but this is a great example. A wonderful woman who does my colonics (yep) in Los Angeles once told me this, "Don't have friends that are overweight. You will become overweight before you help them get skinny." Now of course she was not telling me to be a pompous, arrogant ass, she was just explaining that you are the company you keep. You can help, but don't go eat out with those who don't want to do better.

If you realize, well <u>when</u> you realize that a friend or group of friends are constantly being negative and pulling you down... DUMP 'EM... just that simple. That energy is very powerful and will always affect your Spirit. That law of attraction works every time.

Don't Shut Out Change

So, in the midst of being completely frustrated with this unpredictable weather, I realized that this weather is LIFE. Yes we are in charge of our own destiny, but can we really predict the weather? Do we know when we'll need an umbrella or sunscreen (not in ATL, that's for sure)... all we can do is know that, at some point we will be outside in the thick of it.

Life presents this same understanding, does it not? The trick is, we must learn to dance in the rain and embrace the thunder. Once we do that, storms become the reason behind the Spring. Being from California, I had never endured an entire horrible season, however it has left me with a wonderful experience in change. After the turmoil there is nothing left but your perception; And how you perceive a flood depends on the size of your boat.

My windows are open enjoying the breeze... don't shut out change, even in the rain.

I Want to Get Accustomed to Heaven Now!

Some believe that we're living in hell now. Some believe that hell will come after the second advent of Christ. Some don't believe in hell at all. Well, I believe in Heaven. I believe that there is a time and space, a transition of consciousness and science, where the mind shifts and within that shift is the gloriousness of LOVE, eternal LOVE.

It can be said that that transitional change is currently occurring. Presently the universe is off kilter, transforming and galatically aligning itself for the re-arrival of Spirit. I like to think so are we. That we are off kilter, aligning ourselves for the newness and greatness that is truly us...becoming accustomed to heaven.

See that's what I want. I don't want to be completely shocked out of my mind when I get to Heaven; I want to experience some of it now. I want to taste love, real love. I want to chuckle at the stars, embrace time, fly over my past and converse with God. I want to see everyone's smile even in grief. I want to bless my blessings, know my ancestors, touch my angels and be fulfillingly full...NOW.

I'm not going to wait for that great "Gett'in Up Morning", because I'm UP this morning and today is the day to start becoming accustomed to greatness. Don't settle for anything less than what you give.

So give the greatest part of You!

LET IT GO!

Those three words will change your life. I sat in the presence of a prolific power by the name of Bishop Carlton Pearson who brought forth a word that was so thorough you had to keep standing up so things wouldn't fly over your head. Amongst the large assortment of prophetic things that he said, he, towards the end of the sermon, focused on letting things go. LET IT GO! He then touched on something I write about all the time... Loving yourself.

When you begin to love yourself your perspective of you changes, your perspective of circumstance change and what you allow changes. You realize that you no longer need to be validated by the drama surrounding your life. But you won't realize this until you see your worth... then you WILL LET IT GO.

Let's try it today, right now, even if you're a guy, hug yourself and say I LOVE AND FORGIVE YOU. I almost cry every time I do... must mean I was very hard on myself at one point... wow that's deep.

Love ya!

When you become complacent you become stiff. This is true for every aspect of life. When you don't reach for your goals, you stay at that level of un-achievement. When we don't aim high, we remain in a low life condition. When we don't stretch... we shrivel up and die.

Every morning, STRETCH. Jump out of your bed, touch your toes, lean to one side then the other, reach up to the heavens and pull down today's gifts.

STRETCH out of your comfort zone.

Integrity

As I've been on this journey to become the fullest me, the truest Expression of God (Expression is capitalized for a reason... think about it. WHEW), I realized that I have been entrenched with a-whole-lotta pride... and not the good kind. But because this was the cloth I was wrapped in since birth, I've had great struggles ridding myself of it and even recognizing its presence still in many areas of my life. On Sunday morning I had one of those A-HA moments. People were asked to stand who didn't have their tithe, now that part wasn't the issue, it was the next thing, "God I'm praying for their finances, etc. ..." my pride began roaring like a rabid lion. Then the words, "if there is any place that you should be honest, it's in the House of God." Well I stood my self right on up at that point, fighting this dragon of pride within. Thinking to myself, why do I have this much pride left!? What's the problem?

Gently I said to myself, "You're becoming You; it takes time to be this magnificent." Surely but SURELY, I'm making changes based on the decision I've already made, to be my fullest self, embracing all that I find with kindness, compassion and love.

See I love myself, even the parts I'm changing. Why? Because I know those issues will get changed. I trust myself to be true to myself, my Spirit (Expression) and have faith that whenever I have to fight that lion of pride, I will always win until it is completely destroyed.

Today be completely true to yourself, regardless.

Hey, have a PERFECT *day!*

When Will Your Enoch Come?

Sometimes things must die in order for the replacement to come. I'm not a Bible Scholar but I know it really well, so turn with me (LOL) to Gen. 4:25 and 26 where Adam knew Eve and begat Seth and he begat Enoch... The name Seth actually means "replacement". He was born to replace Abel and through him (the process of), came the entirety of blessing(s). Enoch... that was powerful.

So I'm the little birdie who has come to whisper this in your ear... Let it go. Let it die. We hold on to things, people, situations that we just swear are good for us... and for a time perhaps they were. Then when we loose that which we held so dear, we take forever to let go of the grief. NOW, I'm not one to rush the grieving process, but we can sometimes find ourselves in a revolving slump and never push ourselves back into the world of happenstance(s). When we do this our Seth is never born and our Enoch never comes.

Begin working on allowing that which should die to die off. Let us work on releasing the grief that we've been holding onto for so long... this is the only way our Miracle(s) will be birthed.

LYL LYS!

The Fullest Expression of Myself

When I write I try to allow Spirit to speak through me, for me and to me. My written thoughts are not just a way to encourage others, but it is another form of my expression of me. Last night, while watching Barbra Walters special on Oprah Winfrey (who is one of my favorite persons of all time), she (OW) responded to a question with, “I’m seeking the fullest expression of myself.” I almost passed out! So simplistically profound! DEEP! I almost passed out because that verbiage is always on my lips — Expression.

I am a firm believer that we all are an individual expression of God. Yet a lot of Christians don’t want to hear that and believe I’m headed in the 5%’ers (5 Percenters) direction… And I’m sure we all know I don’t care. We already know, “We are creations that create,” we are much more than we may be too afraid to accept. Nevertheless, we are still just that great.

I vow to continue seeking fullest expression of myself, accepting all that I see of myself, gracefully, passionately and loving every single part of who and what I am.

Divine Intentions Lead to Divine Interventions

WOW! I am truly having some divine appointments in my life these days. It seems like everyone I meet is specifically placed in my life and I in theirs. We all have things in common that we couldn't make up and certainly would not have expected. This morning when I awakened to yet another beautiful day, I thought to myself, this is DIVINE... this is really divine.

I realized that once I grasped my passion, combined it with my purpose, then backed it with good intentions... the universe simply aligned. WOW indeed!

Divine Intentions lead to Divine Interventions - trust me. Today align you goals with your passion and purpose... Then MOVE ON IT...

Take a Step Towards Your Fear

The other side of fear is a beautiful place. Full of calming peace and gentle smiles. Surrounded by a wonderful sense of self. The grass is greener on the other side of that nightmare called fear.

This lack of self-worth, self-empowerment, self-KNOWING or fear, is the main reason, I believe, we don't excel in the areas we so passionately and desperately want to succeed in. For example, I've spoken to thousands of people about weight loss and the trials that come along with it. In some of these conversations I've heard a strong undertone of fear... fear that they will never lose the weight... for various reasons: they physically don't think they can; they've tried before; the addiction to food... etc. All of the reasons are wrapped up in this mind-controlling fright — The "I can't" syndrome.

Take it from me, the first step to getting to that other side is to TAKE A STEP. Whether it's weight, anxiety, crowded places, flying.... whatever it is, you must take a step towards that fear. Sounds crazy but it's the truth. As you began to step towards it, you will grow in yourself, like growing in God). You become a stronger and more confident person. As you get bigger, the fear becomes smaller and smaller until it will make you laugh. You will find yourself hovering over whatever it was that was holding you back... and in that moment you will experience real victory.

So don't be afraid of that bully... GET IN THE GYM. Workout your mind, build muscles in you Spirit, cardio the heck out of your confidence, push-up your self-esteem... eventually that bully will be afraid of you.

Know Your Buttons

Can we really get mad at someone for pissing us off? My answer to this question is No. Energy and vibrations are very real, so when you wear your buttons on your sleeve, expect them to get pushed.

Now what does this mean? GET OVER IT! You didn't think I was going there, huh? Our buttons are simply old wounds that we haven't allowed to heal. I use the word allowed because natural law wants a wound to heal, whether physical or emotional, but we refute that healing process for fear of loosing our identity, our worth, our significance. Whatever it is... whatever the reason... we hold desperately on to that which pains us to even think about. That thought is attracting more attention to the wound, bringing more pain. Bringing more people in, giving even more attention to that sore!

Heal your wounds; Heal your pain; Heal your Spirit! Then no one can tick you off... this is just my thought.

"No man can run from his own story"

This may hurt a little bit.

We've all heard the sayings, "Where ever you go, there you are again." And, "You can't hide from your own shadow". But I have never heard it said quite this way, "No man can run form his own story." That really struck a different chord in me. Not just because it presents a different way of saying, "Stop hiding from yourself" but because it gives ownership to the Writer of that story. You & Me! It brings the attention back to the author and takes it off of the characters within and throughout the story. It also encourages us to remember that we can change and rearrange that which we don't like... in our story. Now here comes the pain...

How many of us are still living last year's.... and the years before story? How many of us still have not lost the 50 lbs. we promised ourselves we would lose at the beginning of this year? How many of us are still in those loveless relationships, have gossipy friendships, work at unbearable workplaces and have dysfunctional mindsets that we were so determined to rid ourselves of? How many of us are hiding from, running away, just trying so desperately to get out of our own story? We have seen it time and time again; that the longer we wait... the longer we wait.

I had an incredible revelation of this very thing. I realized I now write the remaining chapters of my story AND I can and will BASE them off of whatever I choose. Therefore I no longer have to use the previous past experience(s) to be the foundation... I can build a new one. WOW that was an amazing change in my life.

So to all of You out there who are saying, "Wow it's the 8th month in the year and I haven't changed jack!"... You're right, you haven't. BUT YOU CAN! Just get up and do it. It's never too late, because it's always right now.

Creating a Reality That Never Happened

When I was having a horrible time with anxiety, I knew I was "making things up", but couldn't figure out how to stop it. I was constantly grieving over something that never happened and most likely was never going to take place. Finally, after dealing with some things that HAVE taken place in my past I was able to overcome that great hurdle. I was able to really see what's really real. Stop making things up (negative things). Live in the NOW with positive expectations and a perspective of Love... things will always work out that way.

Beware of the toxins in your mind; that's what causes anxiety. When we have toxic thoughts, those thoughts are fatal to all aspects of our lives: relationships, religion, self-love/hate...etc.

Today REPLACE the negative with positive thoughts. Catch the thought and reverse it. Start NOW.

It *Will* Pass

"Keep your head in the exercise."

~ MLM

It reminds me when someone says, "Keep your head in the books"... keep it in focus, keep your head in the game, keep it in the JOY! You have gotten this far by consistency, not by weekly ups and downs!"

I can say this from experience, sometimes life is hard, uncertain, backwards and just a roller coaster. But this too shall pass, it always does - and it is that which keeps us going. For example, in the midst of an anxiety attack a person can feel like they're about to die, literally. But if they can just relax and KNOW that they are not going to die and remember that the last time they had an attack it felt just as bad... and suddenly ... it passed... the feeling will go away as quickly as it came. The same can be said about the daily, weekly, monthly ups and downs we go through. They will pass! Not that it makes it any easier; it just makes you more focused. I have to tell myself often, "Bigger Picture, Megan...Bigger Picture!" This too shall pass.

Be Anxious For Nothing...

Now I get it. I never really liked that verse when I was younger because I didn't understand it. As I got older, I just ignored the verse because I didn't like it. Then this morning as I was meditating and being very honest with God and myself about a situation, I realized that because I was anxious to get something else, I wasn't able to be genuinely grateful for what I just received yesterday! See this is why God owns the cattle on a thousand hills, but He's very cautious about spoiling His kids. I used the word able for a reason. It's almost like a mathematical equation, you can not be grateful while desperately wanting something else, you will come up with a false answer.

This text is not about patience; it's about standing in the midst of thankfulness at all times.

Be grateful, even when you know more blessings are coming... let them come, but saturate yourself in the abundance of now.

What's the Cure

Many times we find ourselves with an ailment that literally debilitates us mentally, emotionally, physically and Spiritually. A story was told of a man who lay on the porch of the CURE (hospital) for 38 years and never went inside to be healed. He had every excuse in the world why he was unable to go those extra two steps to freedom. Finally, one day, Wisdom (doctor) came by and asked him, "Are you READY for your healing?"

That question caused the man to self reflect; "Am I pitting myself? Do I actually like being sick? What am I even sick from?" When he was able to really look at himself and answer these questions he was FREED!

What is the cure for the illness you've been holding on to for decades? Whatever it is the answer is in your DOING SOMETHING ABOUT IT!

Blessing me Right NOW!

Most of us know this song right? *"The Lord is blessin' me, right now, OOOOO right now..."* Well anyone who reads this please go to YouTube and check out Avery Sunshine's version of it.

NOW is the part of this song that makes me smile... I realize that NOW is always a current constant. Right Now is always present. Without the constraints or limits of time, NOW is in-between time itself. Now just left, but is back again without change or movement. So Blessing Me Always...without fail, without cause, without transform... just now.

How does that make you feel? While in trials, circumstances, mystery, are we conscious of the now? The blessings of right now? Let's take a minute and focus on digesting into our systems that "The Lord is Blessing Me, RIGHT NOW". Traditional Buddhist would consider this as a form of being in a constant meditative state; you're conscious of every step you take, or aware of every single thought you have. The Bible puts it this way: Always have a prayer in your heart and on your lips. Imagine the joy we can experience when we concentrate on continued Blessings and not problems.

MAKE IT AWESOME!

Generational Curse

Is it still a curse when you're clear on exactly what's going on? When you aware of the issues that have been passed down from generation to generation; is it still a curse or now a personal challenge? Aunty Oprah says, "When you know better, you do better." I agree with this; However I also believe that in everyone's life there's a fork in the road and at that defining moment YOU decide to be that abusive parent just like your mother, choose to be a drug addict just like your father, OR you say "NO I'm not going to continue this generational curse... it will not find life in mine."

We all have our stories to tell and as it is said, "we all come from dysfunction". But I ask you, WHAT WILL YOU DO ABOUT IT?

Don't let the pink elephant stay in the room next to your children's bunkbeds... fix it now so they won't have to later.

Keep It High

Remember when we were children and the things we did were because we wanted to... because of what we felt? Of course at that age we did not realize the purity of our actions, we just did... we simply just did what we felt. Because of life, those days are pretty much over, we no longer just do, we usually think about everything beforehand. Now I'm not saying that's a bad thing, what I am saying is this; when we were children we did things based on our highest intention.

I found myself being insulted, which is not easy, by what someone was throwing in my face. That's not the point, though. Look here it is: I actually found myself wanting to succeed even more to throw that in their face. WRONG INTENT! I had to sit back and say, "Wait just one minute, chick!" See we've gotten this far in life because of the objectives, the reasons, the purest ideals... those initial passions. Not from jealousy, ill-mannered frustrations and misguided anger.

It is not up to me to prove someone else's wrong... it is up to me to see why it upset me so much and to keep my energy at its highest good. I'm only responsible for myself. I had to stop and keep it on the up and up!

God's Will?

I have been placed on a Women's Prayer email list, where women submit their prayer request and/or Praise Reports. Recently I read a prayer request that asked for healing... "if it's God's will." I found that very interesting. Now I was raised a strict Christian, so I've heard this a number of times, but for some reason it struck me differently today. Who is God? Let me rephrase, "What is God?" He is Love, right? He wants and desires the best for us, so why do we ask for something to be His Will?

The masses preach about God being our Father; better than the father we had or never had. So would your father want you to have cancer and not be healed from it? Would he want you to suffer with a man that is no good, beating you and stealing from you every sense of confidence? Would your father want you to neglect yourself, harm yourself or mistreat your children? I think not.

My mother told me a story a while ago that says: When we get to Heaven there will be a large room full of presents. We will ask God what is this and why didn't I get them on Earth when I needed them? He will answer; "Because you weren't ready to receive them."

Think about this today, tomorrow and whenever you "ask" God for something. Why wouldn't He want you to have whatever it is that you need? 1. Do you really need it? 2. Are you ready to receive it? 3. Are you praising Him in advance for what He's already done? And praise Him BEFORE you ask.

I'm Encouraged

One day I received a response on my blog that rocked me. I was uncomfortable at the thought that someone would actually think that I, me, Megan McGlover would try to take the Glory away from God. Then I received pure encouragement from those who I didn't realize I had affected. God is truly good.

I had to realize that when you're stretching the parameters of thought, consciousness, understandings and awareness you may come up against (should come up against) things that will challenge your own beliefs. You think you going to get all these blessings (gifts from God) and not have to pay for them?. I appreciate God using me as proof of His wonderfully manifested power and LOVE. Use me, until you use me up for the betterment of myself and those who seek the miraculousness of self-empowerment.

I am that I am; And who I am IS an Expression of Love and this reigns true for each and every one of us. Remember that winds may blow, but if you're grounded, they'll never knock you over.

Stand for You

Among many of the places I've spoken, I am honored to say that I spoke in front of the Council of Commerce at the Atlanta Georgia City Hall. I will say however that it was thee topic by which I was monopolized (I think I made that up) and/or beholden to. That is what made it all worth the while. As I went into a wonderful simplistic building in the downtown area of Atlanta, I felt the ambience of Truth, Progression and Affirmative Action in my very bosom... I knew that I was doing the right thing. Rushed through security, then upstairs to sign-in as a speaker, then directed to my seat... the hustle, the bustle... felt too over-rated for someone like me. But then I thought of the cause.

So my thought is this... when you're in your purpose Glory comes. WOW! Let me say that again. When you're in your purpose, living within your destiny, Glory, Praise and Recognition comes, even when you don't want or feel that you deserve it. BE YOU... If you have heard nothing else from me, if nothing else has stirred your Spirit, please remember these words.... BE YOU!

It is you that will fulfill the hopes and dreams of the masses you could never account for. It is YOU that will transform the thoughts of despair and guilt, fear and hopelessness into confidence and structured power! It is YOU, the you that you're not sure about, that will transcend a world of discouragement... it is YOU that we're waiting for.

TODAY BE YOU! STAND for YOU! Stand FOR YOU! Stand for You!

I LYL, I LYS

Do You Cuss When You Pray?

LOL! I was talking to a friend of mine and I told him, "I've learned to be really real when I talk to God." If you can't be real with Him, then you're not even being real with yourself. This is a great controversy among "Christians". I think I'm on to something here. Some would say that it's irreverent; well I say it's all about context. If I'm in the midst of a trial and in pure frustration and I go to God, it is then that His ear is really turned towards me, because I'm at my most sincere point. Same can be said in the midst of praise and joy. When we are at a peak of emotion, God is right there and He already knows what you're thinking, so you might-as-well be YOU- and you just might cuss.

That's just my thought. My relationship with God changed when I realized we are related. WOW! That was deep... Don't miss that one.

WONDERFUL DAY!

Stranded

Reflecting on the crazy snowstorm of 2011 in Atlanta, some of us, like myself are in a house or apartment without any roommates or friends close well within walking distance. The airports are closed and so are most of the roads — we are basically alone. So what can we do with all this time on our hands and how can we keep from developing cabin fever? Get to Know You.

I often talk about *being* what you need, but I suppose if we don't know ourselves, we wont really know what we need. Silence is golden and we're forced to have it surviving storms. Those who are not in the Southeastern states may not be snowed or iced-in however the value is the same. Spend some time getting to know yourself.

Evaluate your transformation. Has there been any? Have you evolved, your wants, desires and dreams? What has changed, are you the same? Write a letter to yourself, talk about those private topics that you never resolved... Be productively alone.

Don't Be Afraid of Freedom

I wonder why we do things that don't feel right to us... so often. Let that sink in for a minute. It seems like we are forever being self-tortured, self-taunted and self-misused. Think about it; we eat things that we know made us sick the last time, but we're going to go ahead and eat it because of blah blah blah... or we don't really like the person we're dating but because blah blah blah... or we hang out with people that are not on the same vibrational wave-length, or we don't like going to church or perhaps that particular church but we go because blah blah blah... the list could go on, right? So why do we continue to punish ourselves? I think it's because we're afraid of change, we're afraid of conflict and we're afraid of freedom.

I realized something; life is kinda like a closet which is usually packed full of stuff! With no room for anything else... well that anything else is the blessing. So don't pack your closet full of stuff that you don't want, it leaves no room. Leave room in your life for something new.

Make the decision today to be HAPPY and to FEEL Joy.

Give It Up … Turn It Loose

I sat with some friends of mine and my Spirit sobbed at the tumultuous atmosphere that had been created. While sitting and listening to them complain about their relationships while putting their mates down, I said to myself, "Wow I've got to pray over this." As the night progressed things became even more grim and I simply felt heavy. But this morning while doing my morning practice, while praying for them, I said, literally, "God, You may have this problem." and I didn't say another word (pertaining to that). Instantly I felt relieved and satisfied. I like that... satisfied.

Giving up that which ails you does not mean that you don't **care**; it means you care about YOU. We can all say we have something that we need to give up and turn loose…

What are you waiting for?

Get rid of it

Be Quiet and Listen

I've only met him once and he is a friend of a friend... therefore I don't know him. I handed him my business card, which I graphically designed myself and he turned his face up so much that he looked like another person, the words, "I'm not feelin' it" was all that came out of his mouth. From that moment, I realized he was yet another person placed in my life for a Divine Intervention/ Interaction. This acquaintance has turned into an advisor literally overnight and I'm more the merrier for it. The product is the proof of the pudding… remember I told you that.

There are times when we think... we just know that what we have is crème-de la-crème and at times it very well could be. But there are other times when it is NOT! This was one of my times and I pray God will continue to put people in my life that will fix those "NOT" moments. As much as I liked my cards, I was able to listen with an open and humble heart to what this man had to say. I was not ashamed that my feelings were hurt, nor were they hurt long. Again, when you're on the path of your PURPOSE, your ego learns to take a back seat, if it wants to stay in the car. (OH that sounds like a MLM quote!)

I'm a woman so I know we have a lot on our minds that we want to express, but when we listen, when we truly shut up and listen the goddess in us shines so fervently, that we no longer need to speak... our beauty makes the point! (another quote... I'm on FIRE!)

Let's quiet our Spirits and listen today.... Shhh "God is try'na tell you something."

FORGIVE YOURSELF

"Well, Megan, you sound ridiculous." Do I? We are our worst critics and we can sometimes treat ourselves like a stranger on the street or worse. When we make mistakes that have lasting affects (like marrying the wrong person, being in a bad relationship for years, gaining a lot of weight and being heavy for years) they can leave us saying, "I can't believe how much time I've wasted." That comment is dangerous. All we can do is recognize our bad choices, evaluate why we made them at that time and simply make a NEW DECISION.

Forgive yourself TODAY don't think about the past anymore.

You Gotta Trim the Fat

Some of us may already know this and some may not... All fat ain't bad. The body actually needs some fat for energy. For example, when a person does not eat, they become very lethargic and drained, because they have no fuel (food). We cannot live on fruits and veggies wholly, we also need carbohydrates and protein AND fat. But all fat ain't good either. Some saturated fats, over processed fats and chemically altered fats not only cause great weight gain, it can present great danger to your overall health.

Some people are there to help and some people have been over processed by life, negatively altered by their past and saturated with simply being unnecessary. Some people provide nourishment and some are weighing you down mentally, emotionally, spiritually and could be physically (if you eat when you're stressed... think about it). Hence we trim the fat. Now trimming the fat is a very good thing, because you don't trim it all, just what you don't need... that excessive waste.

We must realize that our food (our lives) will not loose all flavor (our identity) just because we trim what we were told holds the seasoning (drama)... The meat (truth) is what we really need; all else is there for garnish.

So if you're not enjoying your fat, TRIM IT!

Pat Yourself

So I spoke with someone about being too hard on themselves and it really helped them to understand how self-punishment just spirals into more self-neglect. It's one thing to be focused; it is something else to be so hard on yourself that you can't improve. I think as we live we should always take the time out to congratulate ourselves on the good job we've done so far. Gratitude is key, right?

Think about when we were kids. We always did better when our parents were proud of us, when they nurtured and praised us... I really don't think it changes just because we grow up.

Today... this week, pat yourself on the back; I'm sure you deserve it. I know I do.

LYL LYS!

Did I Get Caught Up?!

I think so, for just a brief moment. "Stoopid News" — one of the segments in my news broadcast on YouTube, is a very funny and popular segment which brings attention to the "non-smart" things that we can sometimes do and the consequences that follow. But that's the point; it brings attention to the negative. I realized this when I was receiving sooo many emails pertaining to stoopid news and the "bad" things that people are doing. I had to step back and take a prophetic look at this. Don't get me wrong, they made my life easier by doing the research for me (I really don't enjoy watching the news AT ALL). However, I felt that I was asking people, subliminally to LOOK for the negative. I would certainly prefer that people LOOK FOR THE POSITIVE. So one night I decided to add a "GOOD NEWS" segment to my broadcast on WMLM- we must always have balance. Because there are children that watch my YouTube videos, I don't want them thinking that the only way to get on my show (by name) or be in the news, is to do something really ignorant. Gotta think about the babies.

What are we really doing with the influence that we have? Are we trying to make the world a better place? Or are we just going with whatever "fits"? I want to do my best at being my best. Ooowwee, I like that. I think I'll say it again. I want to do my best at being my best... I want to be proud of me. So let's think about the affect we have on people we may never meet; co-workers that live in other states, persons that read our blogs, people we talk to on the phone... etc. We may not have this on our minds 24-7, but our energy affects just about everyone we come in contact with one way or another... let's make it a good experience for them.

Fill your life with confidence, high energy, focus and discipline.

To contact Megan McGlover for bookings:

Email: mlm@meganlmcglover.com

Megan is available for Travel, Motivational Speaking, Workshops, Classes, Seminars and Lifestyle Coaching.

For more of Megan's Thoughts:

Youtube Channel: McGloverful

www.meganlmcglover.com

www.justiceforwandamcglover.com

www.ingramcontent.com/pod-product-compliance
Lightning Source LLC
Chambersburg PA
CBHW082103090726
47910CB00008B/2574
9781604148206